How To Get and Keep The Girl you Know you Deserve

I0440842

Copyright 7-2-2012

ISBN: 978-1-300-09664-1

Contents

Prologue

In Today's digital age there are many ways to cultivate a first date but very few explanations on how to create a lasting relationship. So how do you keep that person interested past the weekend? Is it possible to stay in the "love bubble" after year ten? Fifty percent of all couples get a divorce by year ten however this book will keep new and old couples engaged in the relationship for years to come. I give very specific examples and methods on how to woo someone.

Getting a first date is easy especially with Match, EHarmony, Zoosk, and alcohol, but the hard part is to grow a relationship or reawaken one already going on. In case you don't know already I want to point out some points, Match is for people who want to casually date most likely if you are on match you are dating multiple people and just looking to hook up. EHarmony is for someone looking for a long relationship (avg. 3 months.) In order to keep a person interested in a relationship, one must create a lasting impression. The ideas that follow within this book will culminate memorable experiences for years to come.

One day I was searching the internet to try and find a romantic idea for my girlfriend of 4 years. Unfortunately romance is one subject the internet can not help with. I sifted through blogs; top ten lists, and romantic narratives, none of which gave me the romantic ideas I was looking for. My search results consisted of going for walks in the park, visiting museums, or kissing a girl at Fenway stadium. Unfortunately not many girls think Fenway is romantic. So I decided to sit down with nothing but a pen and paper until I could think of a solution. I compiled this list of very specific very romantic ideas that anyone can use. There are ideas for people on first dates and ideas for people who have been married for years. Some of these ideas took me days to think of but have yielded some of the best memories I have.

Chapter I:
Communication

Riddle me this:

Going to the same old dinner can be boring. It's the same routine, same place, same food and most likely the same person. Why not create some excitement and pick somewhere new to eat. Get her excited about it to by telling her where you are going to eat in a new and different way. Do a little research on the new restaurant beforehand. Yelp is a great resource and is able to tell you prices, distance and ratings of restaurants. Once you find the restaurant Google the history of the restaurant. This is important because in the next step you are going to write an email that is a couple of paragraphs long describing the history of the restaurant Let her know if she can guess the place then you will take her there.

Example:

I want to take you out tonight, somewhere you have never been, but if you really want to go with me you have to figure out the restaurant from the clues below.

When we eat I promise I won't shank you but I will probably need a walk in the yard afterwards. Luckily now a day no one watches you eat or pats you down before you go to eat. If this was 20 years ago we would all have to wear the same outfit to dinner. Answer (clink at the liberty hotel)

Paper football:

Do you remember sending notes in high school? By sending funny/quirky notes to each other you are starting your own inside joke and indirectly each person in the relationship will be thinking of the other with anticipation to receive another note. Write the note as if your boss is the "teacher" and your coworkers are the other students. Drop the note in her purse when she's not looking so when she finds it randomly during the day it's a nice surprise. Don't forget to doodle all over the piece of paper; it is supposed to be a "high-school" note. Fold it into a paper football, or if there's time Google how to fold the note into a rose.

Example:

"Late to homeroom again, guess we shouldn't have stayed out late last night but it was totally worth it =)! I was especially sluggish at gym, didn't want to go to gym class but I'd rather be in gym then at a desk doing math all day! People were changing in the locker room and your not going to believe it but the kid who sits next to me all day just gets completely naked and starts talking to me while he's naked. Ummm awkward. Lunch was fun and I got to hang out with Vadim but I think the spaghetti was bad. Can't wait to see you tomorrow this day is just dragging and I really don't want to ……

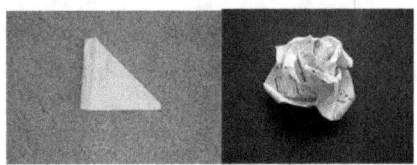

Message in Fiber optics:

The idea behind this is to have her thinking of you. You want to be on the forefront of her thoughts for a couple of days. This is especially important early on in the relationship. One way to do this is to send a coded email. The email can be a simple message or a complex code. If you can make the email more complex, don't use a different language. Simply using a different language is to easy especially with all the "translation" websites on the internet. If she cracks the code within five minutes then you will only be in her thoughts for five minutes. One suggestion is to type the email in a white font so it doesn't show up and looks blank or perhaps a prime number riddle, the first prime number is the letter A, the second prime number is the letter B and so on. My personal favorite is to type a jumble of letters and have one color spell out your message. At the top of the email you can say there's a message coded in my favorite color to see if she can remember what your favorite color is. My favorite color is Green.

XpdaeGbwqsiigagune tnhnloibaspdXpdaeob wqsiigagune tnhnlibaspdXpdaedbwqsiigagu ne tnhnllibaspdXpdaeubwqsiigagune tnhnlci baspdXpdaekbwqsiiXpdaeXpdaeGbwqsiigag une tnhnloibaspdXpdaeobwqsiigagune tnhn libaspdXpdaedbwqsiigagune tnhnllibaspdXp daeubwqsiigagune tnhnlcibaspdXpdaekbwqs iiXpdaeXpdaeGbwqsiigagune tnhnloibaspdX pdaeobwqsiigagune tnhnlibaspdXpdaedbwqs iigagune tnhnllibaspdXpdaeubwqsiigagune t nhnlcibaspdXpdaekbwqsiiXpdaeXpdaek

Video killed the radio star:

Video can also kill the text message. Instead of sending an average dull text message why not record yourself using your cell phone and send it to your loved one. This idea can be modified and used as a sort of scavenger hunt, or this could be used for fun in a game of hide and seek. One way to do this is to send video messages that give clues as to where you are hiding.

Chapter II
A Little More Thought…

A Night In:

Materials:

Fondue extract	Champagne
Strawberries	Oranges
Graham Cracker	Marshmallow
Candles	Movie (Star Dust)
Pot	

This is a classic date that can be done with minimal effort as early as date number three (any earlier and it might be creepy). The idea is to have a chocolate fondue night! I like to get my fondue at either the supermarket; or crate and barrel. Crate and Barrel has higher quality fondue but if you are in a rush the supermarket will work just as well. There are two different types of fondue, microwavable and the one you cook on the stove with crème. If you buy the microwavable fondue still melt it in a pan on the stove. All you have to do is put fondue in a pan and stir until it looks smooth enough to eat. The effort involved in cooking on a stove looks much better to a girl especially if you are still trying to impress her. Light some candles put in a romantic comedy and enjoy.

Backyard Drive in:

Materials:

Mattress	Extension Cords
Television	Blankets
DVD Player	Champaign

On a nice summer night you can put a mattress in the back yard and set up your own private drive in Movie Theater. Pick a romantic movie and pop the wine. It's easy to set up. Just bring a television and DVD player outside via extension cord lie down and enjoy the move. If you still live at home try not to wake your mom up. If you live in the city and don't have a back yard just do some scouting in some rural neighborhoods. Usually you can find a park or something that has outlets that you can use for your television, Medfield is a good nice town with beautiful stars and their parks have readily available outlets.

Message in a book:

Materials:

A book   Know their dreams

Blue Pen

It is important, when on a first date, that you remember specific things the other person says. If for instance someone says they have a dream of opening their own business you should buy them a book on entrepreneurship, and give it to them on the second date. If the person says they like to cook, buy them a cooking book. People enjoy receiving presents, it doesn't matter how much they are but rather how thoughtful they are. I love to give someone a book and circle certain words/letters in the book. The words/letters that are circle in the book spell out a message when they are put in the right order. If you really want to get complex and make this message difficult for her to read you could circle letters that when put together are in another language. This would be extremely difficult to figure out and keep you in the front of her mind for about a week or so as she tries to crack the puzzle. A romantic idea is to have the message give a location and time for the next date.

Another variation for the artist:

Paint by number would be a great message too. Draw out the message and draw shapes around the message and through the message. Have the person you want to decode the paint by number color in the message a specific color so it will POP out when colored.

Wine Olympics:

Materials:

Solo Cups

Wine

Quarters

Small Glass

A Drive to Win!

This game is fun however I don't suggest playing more then 7 times in a row or you may regret trying to go for the gold and end up having someone puke red wine 360 degrees in the bathroom! There are three events in wine Olympics. To set up you need a small cup filled with wine. This glass should have at least four quarters around it. Next you need two solo cups half way filled with wine, and two more solo cups filled to play flip cup. Each person picks a room and hides the solo cup that is halfway filled with wine. The cup must have some portion of it visible but other then that anything goes. To play the game you start off playing flip cup, then run to your assigned room and search for the hidden wine. Once found you have to drink the whole thing before running downstairs and playing quarters. Loser drinks the wine in the quarter's cup and winner has the right to a victory lap around the house.

Chapter III
Thoughtful but Little…

A Dunks Surprise:

It may sound basic but nobody does it. COOK HER BREAKFAST! It shows effort, and girls like to know that you care. Plus nobody ever does it. Even if you don't plan on seeing a girl again COOK HER BREAKFAST, because she has friends and trust me word gets around. If you can't cook feel free to drive out to Dunkin Donuts while she's still asleep. I'm telling you chicks dig breakfast. Another thing I like to do is when you pick her up for a date stop and pick her up an ice coffee without her asking. Be proactive and show that you are thinking of her.

One of these things is not like the other:

This is a fun drinking game to play or it can be a great way to give someone a present. Take two pictures on your phone of the same area. In the second picture have something slightly different like a door ajar or a couch cushion raised up. Just put the gift in the open closet or under the couch cushion. Show the picture to the intended recipient in a completely different room and have them pick out all the differences.

Example:

Mix Tape:

A mix tape or cd is a great way to show you care, and every time she gets in the car and puts on the cd she will be thinking of you. If the wrong song is picked you may be considered creepy and ruin any future chances. When planning what tracks to put on the cd try to consider the below advice.

Don't make all the songs sappy love songs, don't put your voice on the tape/cd, and don't write I love you on the cd anywhere. It is important to show you care just the right amount, so put some songs that you like on the cd and some songs she likes. Ask her what her favorite band is prior to making the tape/cd, When she realizes your remembered what her favorite song is she will be even more impressed.

Get off your Ass:

Physically active dates can be a great way to bond and be healthy. Running with someone can be hard especially since everyone has their own pace but biking on flat land is an easy activity that most women and men can do together. Biking is one of the rare activities that can be done at a relaxing pace for both parties. There are many websites devoted to finding bike paths and they will tell you the type of terrain each trail encompasses. Make certain the terrain is relatively flat.

Providence has an amazing bike path that goes all the way to Bristol. It is seven miles each way and allows the rider to view of the ocean almost the entire seven miles. The ice cream and bistro stops along the way help make this bike path one of the top in the country.

Chapter IV
Large and Expensive

Flower Scavenger Hunt:

Girls love flowers and they enjoy showing /telling their girlfriends about the flowers they received. People know the difference between supermarket flowers and expensive flowers. So it is important to dish out a little extra money and get some expense flowers. One place I like to use that creates a lot of buzz and water cooler talk is Winston flowers in Boston. I like to buy flowers from Winston because I know her friends will comment on the fact that they are from Winston. Hide all twelve roses in different places and write messages on twelve small pieces of paper to go along with each rose. The messages should be personalized and give hints where to find the next rose. Message number twelve can be longer and should include your feelings for her. Sometimes I will give one more location to go to in message twelve and at that location I will have a special gift waiting, like a new purse, theater tickets, or a coupon for a spa day.

Example messages…. "This is the place where you said I love you for the first time… this is the place where we last kissed

Fly Me to The Moon:

Vacations are fun but what every woman wants is to be whisked away. Women want to be swept off their feet and the best way to do this is to plan a vacation without telling her. Call or email your girlfriends boss in advance to request the necessary time off. Stress to her boss the importance of keeping this a secret, the last thing you want is your boss spilling the beans about the secret vacation you have been planning for the past six months. If for some reason you don't think your secret is safe I'm sure your girlfriend will have no problems using a few sick days for a sick vacation. Have a bag packed and in the car for her with all the things you she would need for a getaway. Don't forget the blow dryer and multiple pairs of shoes. For some reason even if the hotel has blow-dryer girls just want to bring their own. The next and last step in this plan is to offer to drive her to work. If you don't work close to each other say you are going in late because you had to run some errands or go to the doctors. When you start driving just take her to the airport. Before she knows what's going on you two will be on your way to a romantic getaway and enjoying those drinks with the little umbrellas in them.

Splash Mountain:

One of my favorite things to do is to write down "I Love You" with an arrow on a piece of paper and keep it in my pocket. If I'm out on the town and I see girls taking pictures I will casually place myself in the picture with the arrow pointing to one of the girls. If you happen to be in Disney World a great way to express your love is a floom ride called Splash Mountain. The ride itself is actually pretty scary but if you sit behind the person you want to share your affections with and take the note out seconds before your picture is taken it is will make for a good story and a romantic picture. At the very least this is a great conversation starter and at the most it's a good way to tell someone you know that you love them. So if there isn't a splash mountain ride around where you live I'm sure you can still find someone to take your picture.

Favorite Date:

Many guys will take a girl to a bar or the movies for the first date. This is a big mistake. It is impossible to learn anything about someone at the movies because there is very little talking. A bar is even worse because the girl will arrive on the date thinking you only want to get her drunk and sleep with her. This makes it much harder to get her drunk and sleep with her. If you happen to be in your mid twenties and single then I'm sure you have a first date you like to "repeat" with girls. My favorite first date has been refined over the years and includes three different locations. It begins with a fancy dinner; I like "pairings" in Boston. At this restaurant they pair your food with a specialty wine, and are also well known for their great service. Next I like to go across the street to a comedy club called "Dick Doherty's" they have comedy shows every night and at a very reasonable price. After the comedy show you can walk through the commons and head to Finale's it's a dessert only restaurant but don't worry because they also serve wine. This date is guaranteed gold; but a slightly cheaper version is to start off at legal test kitchen with one dollar pbr's and nice food. Legal test kitchen is a testing restaurant for the Nationwide Legal Sea Foods restaurant and is quite excellent.

Floor seats:

Buying floor seats can be expensive but it is definitely worth wild. The trick in the beginning of any relationship is to stand out and differentiate yourself from all the other dates she's ever been on. One way to differentiate yourself is to do something the other person has never done before. Buying floor seats to a sports game, especially if the other person knows nothing about the sport, will create a great memory and a lasting impression. Explaining the way a game is played helps both of you connect and shows her that you can be patient, understanding, and able to share things from your life with her. Also floor seats help because she probably has never had seats that close to any sporting event before. The seats will make her feel important and show her how much she means to you. Tell her that you have never been in seats that close before either, Girls love it when you are both experiencing new things together.

Chapter V
Why Not?

Trench coats and heals:

Why not ask to be surprised? Having a girlfriend show up in nothing but a trench coat and heels is extremely sexy for both you and her. Just make sure your roommate is out of town that weekend. You can dress up for her some nights too. You may want to stay away from the heels though, and go to a Halloween shop or amazon to purchase your costume. A police officer's uniform with handcuffs can be fun. The only step left is to show up unannounced!

Make dinner:

A good recipe for dinner would be oysters with a white wine sauce. Go to Google and search for oyster recipes online. You will see this is a fairly simple aphrodisiac to cook. Trader Joes sells two dollar bottles of wine so you don't have to spend a fortune on the wine. This is a cheaper date but is still a lot of fun. If the girl you are dating likes Italian food make cannelloni instead of oysters, if she likes American you can try cola chicken. Cola chicken is by far one of the easiest things to make. It takes 45 minutes to cook which gives the impression that you are really putting a lot of effort into cooking dinner. Also with cola chicken you are making your own barbeque sauce which is a great conversation starter, it also gives you plenty of time to taste all those wines.

Cinderella's Ball:

The dream of finding prince charming still exists in every woman's head and heart. Girls want to be taken out and treated like a Disney Princess. One way to do this is to take them to a ball. There are many charity events through the year and some are fairly inexpensive. One event that you can get tickets to is called Santa Clause anonymous. It's a black tie event that happens every year around Christmas time and is only about fifty dollars a ticket. There is a live band, lots of dancing and even some casino games. If you volunteer for an hour during the ball the ticket price drops even more. Be sure to rent a hotel room and go all out, as it is supposed to be a romantic night where you treat her like a Disney Princess.

Wine Tasting

Buy 5 or six different wines and host your own wine tasting. Choose three reds and three whites. This way you guarantee to have at least one type of wine everyone likes. Cover up the labels on the wine bottles with your most awkward pairs of boxer shorts. Using your boxer shorts to cover up the labels of the wine bottles is awkward but it will defiantly start a conversation. If you can sense the boxer short trick is hurting you just say your roommate or friend put boxer shorts on the wine bottles as a practical joke and then apologize for his immaturity. This makes you look more mature. This is also a great date to share with another couple and can be easily made into a competition between couples.

Chapter VI
Classic Valentine's Day Ideas

Hand Written Card:

Do you Remember Valentine's Day in grade school? Everyone had a brown paper bag hanging from their desks and you would drop off a special valentine card in the bag of the person you really liked? It might have been special because it had a Hershey Kiss attached to it or you might have written an extra special message on the back of the card. Back then we would put a lot more thought about exactly what to say and designing a card. We didn't have any money to buy a specialized card with music from Hallmark; we had to create our own cards. The cards you give today should have the same thought they did when you were in elementary school. They should be well thought out and different from all the other cards. Draw out a card, and if you can't draw then trace something. Find out something they like. If they like Disney World then draw out Mickey and Minnie kissing on the Front. If they like Dunkin Donuts put a 10 dollar gift card in it. It's the small stuff that counts and the stuff that gets you noticed and in her head.

Singing the Blues:

Develop a song for that special someone. If you can't play an instrument there are three "work arounds" to cover up this inability. The first option is to ask a friend to play an instrument while you sing. The second work around is to strike all the strings on a guitar in a particular rhythm like a blues rhythm. Then set lyrics to that rhythm. Your final option is to develop your own lyrics to go along with the music of a song that's already been created. Record your song on an mp3 or use an app to pair your voice and the music together. Whatever option is taken it is important to note that the song is played at exactly the right time. Valentine's Day would be a great time to take advantage and debut your first song. Before you go out with your date for the evening, decorate a gazebo with all white Christmas lights. Write the words "I love you" with white Christmas lights in some trees next to the gazebo. When you arrive with your date play the song on your car radio and ask her to dance. Be assured even if you can't sing it will still be magical.

Meaning of Pedals

Each rose has a specific meaning one of the more rare colors, and hardly ever seen is the purple rose. The innovation of the purple rose was to symbolize enchantment. You give a purple rose to convey that you have fallen in love with the recipient at first sight. Not many people know the meaning of roses which works is great. This makes you seem more romantic and sensitive. Once you explain the meaning she will always remember what the purple rose. From this moment on you may have to be careful what color flowers you do give because she will certainly go on Google to look at what each flower signifies.

It's about being together:

Horseback riding is always a fun activity to do together. If you don't want to ride horses then just do something out of the ordinary. It could even be as simple as playing a bored game together; having a picnic on the beach. Some of my favorite moments are just lying in bed and looking into the soul of a loved one and just having her next to me. Try to schedule some time each day to just be together with no distractions or stresses, and try to leave any topics that could be stressful like money or work out of the conversation.

Weekend Pass:

Create a weekend pass coupon. It should say "weekend getaway" and notate the distance this pass is good for. Notating the distance is a good idea because her immediate thought may be weekend getaway to Italy! The reason behind a weekend pass is to help communication, she can give the pass to you when she feels stressed out, and this is a great way to help pick up on her feelings. Women think we should just know how they feel, but if you give them this coupon they are indirectly telling you how they feel. This will lead to less stress and a happier relationship overall.

A Cruise to Nowhere:

One of the most romantic things can be surprise weekend trip to nowhere. In many cities they have cruise ships that will go to sea for a couple of nights and then come back to port. They are fairly inexpensive and well worth the time away. This would be an especially great idea if you date has never been on a cruise before. It's all the luxury without all the cost.

The One Knee I Love You:

Find a secret place, it might take you a few hours on Google or if you can remember a secluded special romantic place then go there with your date. Get down on one knee and tell her you are not asking her to marry you but you just wanted to show to her how much you love her and how happy she makes you every day. I like to be specific as possible so I did some research and found there are some secret gardens at the Louvre, in Paris that are only open part of the year. There are marble statues inside and the perfect place to tell someone you love them. Also if you can find the wishing well in the Magic Kingdom then you just found one of the most romantic spots in the entire kingdom.

Chapter VII
Final Bit of Advice

The First Kiss:

Finding a romantic spot for your first kiss is a big mistake. If you take your date out and things become too romantic to early you may scare your date off. Boston.com lists Fenway Stadium as one of the top spots for first kisses however I believe Fenway is to public and can lead to an embarrassing rejection. Unlike Boston.com I also believe that the first kiss has to be on that first date. It is the deciding factor between the friend zone and something more. If it is coming to the end of the night and you are dropping someone off you better go in for a kiss before they leave the car otherwise you may find her only thinking of you as a friend. If the kiss is terrible the first time don't worry, because it may become a memorable experience you can share together for years to come, and laugh about with friends.

The Bars:

Bars are like going the beach and not being able to talk. You are judged in a split second by a lot of people and the music is so loud it is impossible for anyone to judge you on more than your looks. Also picking people up at bars can be extremely hard. The competition is fierce and innumerable. You are better off going to a party with friends where everyone is a friend of everyone. At the Bars you have to compete with guys who are 23 go to school and have time to work out all day every day. Or you may have to compete with guys who are much richer then you have better close and orders everyone drinks. It can be extremely hard to talk to anyone especially if the bar is blaring music. Girls also go to the bars in packs so breaking into a pack and getting approval from her 10 friends can be extremely difficult. If you want to meet someone stay away from bars, if you want to get drunk go to a bar.

Hat trick:

Try not to wear a hat, especially on a first date. Your date wants to see what you look like; she doesn't want to know you're so insecure you can't even go on a first date without your hat. If you wear a hat your date will think one of three things. She may think you are too insecure to leave home without your hat or you're just ugly with your hat off. Even worse she may think you don't care about the date enough to brush your hair. Take off your hat when you meet her parents or even her friends, especially if you are having a meal with them towards the beginning of the relationship. Everyone notices when you wear a hat!

Routine:

We all have routines and certain activities we keep
repeating over and over again. The trick to mastering
any relationships is to try and experience things you
normally wouldn't experience. Step out of your
comfort zone and do activities your date wants to do.
These activities might not be the things that you
normally enjoy and it may be hard to get excited about
these activities but try to <u>act</u> excited for your date.
Some of these activities may include art museums, dish
washing, car shopping, or watching her perform in an
equestrian competition. Trying new things and breaking
your routine is especially important early on in a
relationship. Your date wants to know you are exciting
and adventurous. She doesn't want to date the guy who
orders a bacon cheeseburger and fries every night for
dinner so instead of ordering the burger and fries, why
not try the calamari, she is sure to comment on your
great selection.

The 17 and under crowd:

Obviously if you're still in high school some of the ideas in this just wont work and should not be tried. You certainly can't take someone away on a trip or afford to take them to floor seats at a basketball game. I found when you are in high school only one thing matters to girls, and that is how cool you are. If you're not cool at your school don't worry there are ways to fake it, and also ways to get that first kiss if you still haven't gotten one yet.

If you're not cool at your school then go to a school dance with a buddy at a different school. Make sure its not your school. The people in your school have known you since you were five so if it hasn't worked out for you their by now chances are its not going to magically start working out for you. Try to find a friend of a friend or someone at a different school so you can get an invitation to their school dance. If you don't have any friends at different schools call up random schools and ask when the next dance is. It's a bold move but has to be done!

In the next step you want to find someone you want to dance with. Sounds simple enough but DON'T DANCE WITH HER! Chances are she's hot popular and everyone wants to dance with her so there's no way! What you want to do is dance with someone that is much hotter then her but make it so she can still see who you are dancing with. I bet your asking right now if you can't get the uglier girl how are you going to dance with the hot one? Simple, just tell the hot girl the truth. Tell her you really like the girl you picked out earlier and you want to make her jealous. Surprisingly this always works. The next part is easy.

Dance, and look like you're having fun. When the dance is over ask the girl that you like to dance. When that song is over ask her to dance again and try to keep dancing up for at least 3 songs. After you dance ask her if she wants to grab a soda, this is your time to tell her a witty story about yourself so make sure it's a good one. After that your basically home free, however one note of caution when you do dance make sure you don't grind on either girl unless she initiates it, surprisingly girls don't like it when you rub your junk on their leg without being asked.

Friends:

Try to make friends with neighbors and friends of friends. You really should increase your social circle. Having a large number of friends provides you with more opportunity to meet new people while providing a support system while you are out with a new person. One way to meet new people is to throw a party and let people know they should bring guests. Don't be afraid to play silly games like truth or dare, or if your old enough kings. It helps lighten the mood, and gets everyone to know each other in a fun atmosphere.

"To Fall for Love can lead to falling in Love"

Forever and Always

John F. Olivieri III

www.ingramcontent.com/pod-product-compliance
Lightning Source LLC
Chambersburg PA
CBHW071306280526
45788CB00004B/1848